The Mar in the Moon

One bright sunny day,
the man in the moon
went to have fun
in the afternoon.

"This is fun!" said the man in the moon as he went for a ride in a hot-air balloon.

Oh no! Be careful. Here comes trouble. Guess what's coming on the double...

4

A whirling, twirling
wind came by.

7

Fun in the Sun

"This is fun!" said the man in the moon as he dived into the blue lagoon.

Oh no! Be careful. Here comes trouble. Guess what's coming on the double...

8

A crunching, munching
shark came by.

Guess What's Coming

"This is fun!" said the man in the moon as he played around on a sandy dune.

Oh no! Be careful. Here comes trouble. Guess what's coming on the double...

12

A catching, snatching fisherman came by.

Fun in the Sun

"This is fun!" said the man in the moon as he caught a fish with a wooden spoon.

Oh no! Be careful. Here comes trouble. Guess what's coming on the double...

17

A whooshing, swooshing
storm came by.

19

Fun in the Sun

"This is fun!" said the man in the moon as he bounced around inside a monsoon.

Oh no! Be careful. Here comes trouble. Guess what's coming on the double...

"Night is coming," said the man in the moon. "I'll have to go to work very soon."

Oh no! Be careful. Here comes trouble. Guess what's coming on the double...

23

The sizzling, grizzling
sun came by.
"The man in the moon
had fun all day.
Now it's night,
and it's my turn to play!"